IMAGES OF AIR WAR 1939-45

IMAGES OF AIR WAR 1939-45

Chaz Bowyer

B. T. BATSFORD LTD · LONDON

Contents

Page 1   Bloch 152s of the French air force, spring 1940, believed to be from 8 *Escadrille, SPA 94* (*'Whispering Death'*) of GC II/1; virtually the best French fighter available then in any significant quantity for first-line operations. *(J. Cuny)*

Previous page   Good luck. Airmen and airwomen giving the thumbs-up greeting to Lancasters as they take off for a night operation.

ISBN 0 7134 3784 7

Typeset by Tek·Art Ltd
and printed in Great Britain by
Butler & Tanner Ltd
Frome, Somerset
for the publishers B. T. Batsford Ltd, 4 Fitzhardinge Street,
London W1H 0AH.

By the same author
Calshot, 1913-61
The Flying Elephants
Mosquito at War
Hurricane at War
Airmen of World War One
Sunderland at War
Hampden Special
Beaufighter at War
Path Finders at War
Albert Ball, VC
For Valour – The Air VCs
Sopwith Camel – King of Combat
History of the RAF, 1912-77
Guns in the Sky – The Air Gunners
Coastal Command at War
Fighter Command, 1936-68
Spitfire
Veteran Aircraft of WW2
Bomber Group at War
Age of the Biplane
Desert Air Force at War (co-author)
Air War over Europe, 1939-45
Encyclopaedia of British Military Aircraft
Lancaster
Hurricane
Wellington at War

Introduction

Two points must be emphasised to any reader of this book. First, it is in no way intended to masquerade as any form of 'history' of the aerial conflict of 1939-45. Secondly – and especially – it is *never* this author's goal to glorify war in any shape or facet. To me, all wars are summed succinctly in an old Service cliché – 'War is not a matter of who is right – but who is left . . . .'

Instead, I have attempted here to offer a pictorial 'savouring' of the air war of World War II; an esoteric re-creation of the atmosphere of those fateful years from an airman's viewpoint. Inevitably, perhaps, a single slim volume must omit myriad subjects and facets of such a broad concept; hence I have deliberately given more space to what I term the human side of that war. Old men make wars, but it is always the young generation of any nation which actually has to fight, placing unfulfilled futures in constant jeopardy and – so often – making the supreme self-sacrifice.

Chaz Bowyer
Norwich, 1982

Fighter aces of the USAAF's Eighth Air Force, based in England. From left: Col Francis Gabreski; Capt Walter V. Cook; Capt Robert Johnson; Lt-Col David Schilling (behind Johnson); Capt 'Bud' Mahurin; Col Robert B. Landry. *(USAF)*

Awakening

When the European war erupted in September 1939, the air forces of each country immediately involved were by no means properly equipped or wholly prepared to undertake any extended form of aerial offensive, or defensive, operations against any other air service. The British Royal Air Force had begun a hasty expansion and modernisation programme only within the previous five years, the fruits of which had yet to ripen. Up-to-date fighter aircraft designs – best represented by the Hawker Hurricane and Supermarine Spitfire – had only relatively recently begun to replace outmoded biplanes on first-line squadrons. RAF Bomber Command was wholly equipped with twin- or single-engined aircraft, each carrying modest bomb loads over medium ranges, of mediocre performance, and with poor defensive armament. As an island, Britain's vital dependency on imported goods and materials was considered adequately protected by the might of the Royal Navy; aerial protection in the guise of RAF Coastal Command at that time comprising a heterogeneous collection of almost 450 aircraft – two-thirds of this 'strength' being slow twin-engined Avro Ansons of very limited operational range. In total, the RAF could claim 157 squadrons – nearly 2000 first-line aircraft, with almost 8000 more 'in reserve' – by 1 September 1939. Of these, 34 squadrons were scattered abroad throughout the British Empire, while 28 squadrons were still biplane-equipped. For UK defence, 400 Hurricanes and 270 Spitfires – but the rest of Fighter Command consisted of 'converted' Blenheim I fighters and outdated biplanes.

Despite a massive propaganda campaign over several years, the RAF's chief future opponent, the German Luftwaffe, was, at that period, little better fitted or prepared for any prolonged air war. From its secret genesis in 1925, the Luftwaffe had been created on a narrow platform of purely tactical air power; an integral adjunct to the German armies, with no provision for any separate existence as a strategical force in its own right. Its aircraft were standardised in design to a high degree to meet short-term tactical requirements. Apart from its standard first-line fighter, the Messerschmitt Bf 109, which was on a par or superior to any other fighter in the world, the Luftwaffe was equipped with such barely adequate designs as the Heinkel He III, Dornier Do 17/215, and Junkers Ju 87 as its bomber arm – all of relatively poor operational potential. Like the RAF at that period, the Luftwaffe possessed no four-engined, heavy, strategic bomber, but while the RAF already had long-term provision for an eventual 'all-heavy' bomber force in a well-advanced stage, the Luftwaffe had only the Heinkel He 177 bomber in prospect, which did not enter operational service until late 1942 and had no significant impact on the aerial conflict. The most accurate figures available indicate that on the eve of war the Luftwaffe possessed a gross total of slightly over 4000 aircraft 'available'; though no more than 90 per cent of these could truly be classified as immediately operational.

Of the other nations quickly to be embroiled in the air war against Germany, France's air services were collectively the largest in quantity of aircraft – close to 4000 machines of every type and role – yet due to years of French bureaucracy and political vacillation, were hopelessly obsolete in overall equipment. Its nationalised aviation industry failed to deliver promised quantities of more updated designs, while American and British-designed aircraft ordered to fill the gaps failed to materialise in any significant numbers before May 1940 when France was invaded by Germany. The Polish air force – the first to oppose the Luftwaffe – had equally suffered from political indifference to air power for many years; even the Polish army's cavalry had been allotted twice the financial budget given to the PAF. On 1 September 1939, when Germany launched its military might against Poland, the PAF could muster a total of only 396 combat aircraft, of which 156 were defending fighters of obsolescent concept.

On 10 May 1940, after months of relatively relaxed operations during the popularly dubbed 'Phoney War' period, the Luftwaffe spearheaded a massive German assault against France and the Low Countries. It was a brilliantly planned three-pronged attack. Two prongs were aerial assaults against Belgium and Holland, as insurance against possible 'flank' interference to the main thrust, against France. The Belgian air force – less than 200 aircraft of all types – had over half of these destroyed on the ground in the first German onslaught; while the Dutch air service, with a mere 130 available aircraft, was overwhelmed within five days. Luftwaffe strength on that fateful day exceeded 3500 aircraft; while opposing the central invasion of France were just seven RAF fighter squadrons (supplemented by three more on 11 May from England), plus some 250 RAF bombers and 'army co-operation' aircraft, apart from the ill-matched French fighters and bombers. The eventual outcome was – tragically – predictable. By 4 June 1940 effective Anglo-French resistance had

Before the storm. Hawker Hurricane, PD-P, of No.87 Sqn RAF at Debden during the August 1939 peacetime annual exercises – only days before the 'real thing' erupted.

Left Messerschmitt Bf 109 fighters of the Luftwaffe dispersed during a prewar war game.

to all intents ceased, and within three weeks France formally surrendered.

The aerial cost of Germany's highly successful *blitzkrieg* offensive was high for all participating air services. From 10 May to 4 June, the RAF lost totals of 432 Hurricanes (mainly), Spitfires, and other fighters; while the overall RAF loss figure for the whole *blitzkrieg* period amounted to almost 1000 aircraft of all types – the equivalent of almost 40 operational squadrons. The Luftwaffe too had suffered high casualties – at least 1300 aircraft lost on operations, while almost as many again were categorised as in need of extensive repair or replacement. Nevertheless, the Luftwaffe now occupied airfields and bases along the northern French and Baltic coasts, as well as Norway, all within reasonably easy striking range of Britain; the scene was now set for an aerial battle which would prove to be a significant turning point in the Luftwaffe's fortunes and in the conduct of the war. Pure aerial power was about to be entrusted with a responsibility unique in military aviation history. The Battle of Britain was about to commence.

Top Hurricane I, N2358, 'Z' of No.1 Sqn RAF in France, late 1939.

Above Fairey Battle bombers – a 226 Sqn machine is illustrated – formed the equipment of ten RAF squadrons (160 aircraft) sent to France on 2 September 1939. Poorly armed, and of mediocre performance, the Battle units were virtually massacred in May 1940, when the German services made their main attack against France and the Low Countries.

Rotterdam vista after the Luftwaffe's mid-day attack on 14 May 1940. This area was the Binnenstad old town and port, while the 15th Century Groote Kerk seems to point an accusing finger at the skies.

Right Poignant remains of a Belgian Air Force Hawker Hurricane, at Schaffen-Diest airfield; destroyed on the morning of 10 May 1940 by a surprise Luftwaffe strafing sortie. *(AELR Air Museum, Brussels)*

Below Another victim of the initial *Blitzkrieg* assault by German forces against France, on 10 May 1940. Fairey Battle L5540, JN-C of No.150 Sqn RAF, brought down during an attack on bridges across the Meuse.

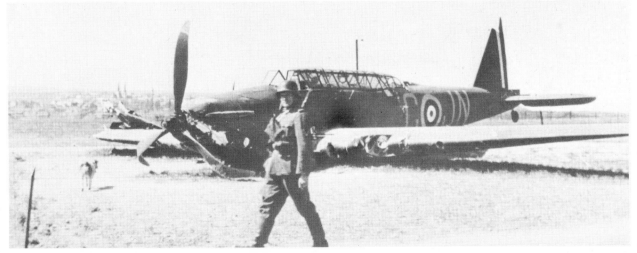

Clash of Eagles

The Battle of Britain is now recognised primarily as a battle solely decided by air power – the first such in history – but also as a watershed in the fortunes of Göring's much-vaunted Luftwaffe. Until June/July 1940, the German air force had virtually swept all before it, bolstering a myth of near-invincibility so carefully fostered by Göring in pre-war years. The battle also revealed Göring's utter failure to appreciate the correct use of air power. Unlike past classic military battles, the struggle had no specific 'zero hour' for commencement, though officialdom in Britain later found it convenient to lay down official parameters to the Battle of Britain as commencing at 0001 hours on 10 July 1940 and ceasing on 2359 hours on 31 October 1940. This arbitrary selection of dates, however, ignores the significant 'overture' operations by both the RAF and the Luftwaffe in June and early July that year, while the night bombing campaign pursued by the Luftwaffe against Britain throughout the winter of 1940-41 was, as far as the Luftwaffe was concerned, the final phase of their aerial assault.

With the defeat of France in June 1940, and the retrieval of Allied troops via Dunkirk, Britain now stood alone, facing the almost-certain possibility of a German invasion and occupation as the next move in Hitler's bid for total domination of Europe. The prime responsibility for the defence of the United Kingdom lay in the capable hands of Air Chief Marshal Sir Hugh Dowding, commander of RAF Fighter Command. The disastrous preceding campaigns in Norway and France had already reduced his Command's strength in seasoned pilots and fighter aircraft to a dangerously low figure, so that on 30 June he could count on a total of only 1200 pilots and slightly less than 600 fighter aircraft immediately fit for operations. These figures were to improve weekly throughout the subsequent battle, but never more than by 25 per cent. One huge asset for the UK defences was the chain of radar posts spread along England's southern and eastern coasts; a pre-intelligence system able to plot incoming raiders and thus allow Fighter Command a high degree of tactical advantage in placing defending formations. By July 1940 this radar chain comprised 51 such 'listening' posts.

Across the Channel the Luftwaffe, on 20 July, could muster nearly 2000 bombers and fighters for the intended assault on Britain; this onslaught being aimed at gaining total air supremacy as a vital prerequisite to a planned seaborne and airborne invasion of England. Göring's boast, that the RAF

fighter force would be destroyed on the ground and in the air '. . . within two or three days', sounded feasible, if pure superiority in numbers was the criterion. This fallacy was soon cruelly shattered. The 'opening' period from 10 to 31 July saw the RAF mount some 12,000 individual fighter sorties, shooting down 270 German aircraft, but losing 145 British fighter aircraft. Of the latter, 51 pilots were killed, and 18 others wounded, injured or incapacitated. It was initially a specific attempt by the Luftwaffe to create a battle of pure attrition, whereby sheer numerical strength would ultimately prevail. In fact, as casualty lists indicate, the Luftwaffe was losing nearly 20 times as many air crew members as the RAF.

During August Göring switched his offensive to an all-out attempt to destroy the main RAF fighter stations in southeast England, and indeed had almost reached a point of succeeding in his aim when, on 7

Left Gegen England. Heinkel He 111 bombers en route across the Channel, 1940.

Above Hurricane pilot of 87 Sqn RAF – symbolising the legendary 'Few' who faced the might of Göring's Luftwaffe in the fateful summer months of 1940. *(British Official)*

September, he switched again, directing his Luftwaffe to concentrate on massive day raids directly against London only. In fact, this extraordinary decision had come direct from Hitler, who wanted revenge for a series of RAF bombing raids on Berlin during four recent nights. For Fighter Command this decision meant a relatively simpler task thereafter, concentrating in the main on protecting a single objective, London. With improving supplies of fresh aircraft and pilots, the Command became embroiled in several weeks of savage fighting, tackling huge bomber formations and their fighter escorts en route to the English capital; reaching a virtual peak of intensity on 15 September – the day now allotted annually for Battle of Britain remembrance ceremonials, displays and services. On that date the RAF destroyed 60 German aircraft and crippled dozens of others. Its own losses were 26 fighters, though 13 of their pilots were retrieved to fight on. Two days later, Hitler issued a personal order postponing Operation Sealion – the intended invasion of Britain.

By November 1940 the vast daylight aerial struggle had petered out, as the Luftwaffe directed its energies into the night *blitz* against British cities and industrial centres. Overall, the cost in lives and aircraft throughout the Battle had been grievous. The RAF

had lost 481 pilots killed or missing, with a further 422 wounded, burned or otherwise injured; virtually one in three of all participating pilots. Aircraft lost amounted to 1140, but these could easily be replaced. The Luftwaffe had lost 1733 aircraft and their crews, apart from almost 650 others severely damaged. Those RAF pilots who had fought came to be dubbed 'The Few' by the British Prime Minister, Winston Churchill – and some 800 of those who survived the Battle were destined to be killed on operations later in the war. Their courage, skills, and constant refusal to be daunted by overwhelming odds ensured the freedom of a nation in the fateful summer months of 1940.

Left Spitfire pilots of No.610 Sqn, Auxiliary Air Force at immediate 'Readiness' state, Biggin Hill, 1940.

Left, below Wings over Westminster. Fighter contrails above Big Ben in September 1940, recalling Stephen Spender's lines, '. . . and left the vivid air signed with their honour' . . . .

Right Return from combat. Hurricanes of No.32 Sqn RAF landing at Biggin Hill on 15 August 1940, at the height of the Battle of Britain.

Now thrive the armourers . . . . Spitfire 1a of No.19 Sqn RAF being quickly rearmed and replenished for further combat, Duxford, 1940. Note 'blown' fabric-patch coverings to the wing-guns' ports, indicating fired guns. *(Imperial War Museum, CH 1367)*

Right Aerial combat is a young man's game – exemplified by these young Luftwaffe bomber crew members shot down over England, summer 1940.

Experten – the German idiom for fighter 'aces'. Generaloberst Ernst Udet (centre) visits Luftwaffe fighter pilots on the Channel Front, 4 September 1940. From left, these were Balthasar, Oesau, Adolf Galland, Werner Mölders, unknown, Grasser. Four of these aces were destined to die later in the war.

Below 'I gave him a two-seconds burst and his starboard engine erupted' – a Heinkel 111 bomber 'buys it', summer 1940. *(British Official)*

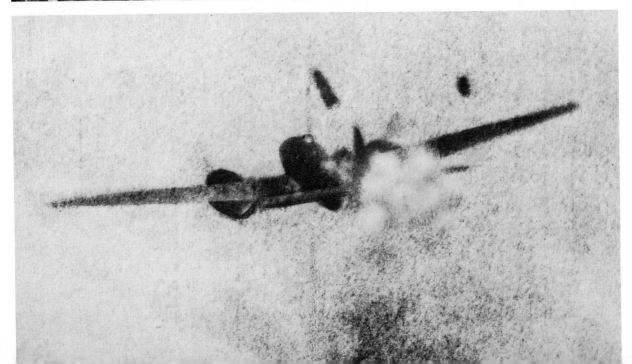

On 30 September 1940, Oberleutnant Karl Fischer of 7/JG27 dived on two unarmed Avro Anson training aircraft, but stalled on a steep turn and crashed in Windsor Great Park. Here, his Messerschmitt Bf 109E is being salvaged.

Left, above Havoc in a typical London street after a Luftwaffe night raid – a sight increasingly familiar to city commuters during the winter of 1940-41.

Left Italian Fiat BR20 bomber of 243 Squadriglia, 99 Gruppo, 43 Stormo shot down by Plt Off Graham Leggett of No.46 Sqn RAF, which crashed in Rendlesham Forest, Suffolk, on 11 November 1940.

Above Scoreboard. Sqn Ldr Peter Townsend, DFC (kneeling), with other pilots of No.85 Sqn RAF (Hurricanes), and the unit 'kill tally' marked on a German propeller from one of the squadron's victims.

Right Veteran. Squadron Leader B.J. 'Sandy' Lane, DFC, who commanded No.19 Sqn RAF (Spitfires) during the Battle of Britain. He was killed in action the following year.

Bomber Assault

The true 'spine' of all aerial warfare during World War II was the bomber. Fighters, flying boats, photo-reconnaissance machines, *et al* – all played their vital roles; but only the bomber could extend the long arm of offensive strategy, paving the path to ultimate victory. Such an offensive could only be able to be mounted throughout the war by, primarily, the RAF and, from 1943, the USAAF. Both forces had planned eventual bomber arms equipped with four-engined, heavy, long-range aircraft to implement true bombing strategic offensives against Germany and its Italian and Japanese Axis partners. The Luftwaffe possessed no such bomber force, having been originally created solely as a *tactical* accessory to the German armies; a flying artillery to spearhead Hitler's favoured *blitzkrieg* ('lightning war') method of warfare and conquest. No four-engined, heavy bomber force was available until 1943, and then only in insignificant numbers. It was an omission in long-term strategy overtly revealed during the 1940 attempt to crush Britain, and a gap in Luftwaffe offensive capability which was never filled.

The years 1939-42 saw the RAF still awaiting re-equipment of its firstline bomber force with the planned 'heavies' in sufficient strength to pursue its strategic offensive against the Reich. In the interim it 'soldiered' on with twin-engined Hampdens, Blenheims, Wellingtons and Whitleys – all prewar designs of relatively restricted capabilities – suffering high casualties for relatively little success. The introduction of the Stirling, Halifax, and Avro Lancaster to operations by the close of 1942 finally offered the opportunity to augment the offensive, aided by improved radio and radar navigational and bombing equipment for improved accuracy in locating and destroying any objective. By then too the disastrous policy of despatching unescorted bombers on daylight operations prevalent during 1939-41 had been changed by the RAF to a night offensive only. The year 1942 also heralded a fresh threat to Germany when the first elements of the USAAF's Eighth Air Force arrived at bases in

England; harbingers of a planned ultimate force of 3500 US bombers and fighters to be available in England by mid-1943. The USAAF's policy for its heavy bomber force of Boeing B-17s and Consolidated B-24s was a stubborn determination to prove the worth of *daylight* bombing; a policy it adhered to until the cessation of hostilities in 1945. The first year of such USAAF missions incurred appalling casualty rates – as such a policy had to the RAF in its early years of similar operations – but these did not deter the American hierarchy from its goal.

With increasing strength in numbers of heavy bombers, and continuing improvements in technical aids, the Allied bombing attacks against Germany intensified throughout 1943-4. By then the German nightfighter and anti-aircraft gun defences had also improved, and the consequent night and day clashes in German skies assumed proportions unprecedented in aviation history. Bomber streams of 800-900 bombers on a single operation became a common practice, and individual targets, such as the cities of

Hamburg and Berlin, were singled out for concentrated attacks, resulting in depths of horrific destruction unknown before in war. A measure of the efforts – and sacrifices – of RAF Bomber Command at this period can be illustrated by the facts. From April 1943 to the end of March 1944, the bomber crews flew a total of 69,548 individual sorties. From these, 2703 aircraft failed to return, the equivalent of almost 19,000 crew men killed or prisoners of war, or the strength on paper of 130 Lancaster squadrons.

In the months preceding 6 June 1944 – the first day of the Allied invasion of Normandy – the Allied bomber forces were 'diverted' from their main role of pounding Germany to help 'prepare' the ground for the invasion ground forces. By then Allied air supremacy over France made it possible for the Allied bombers to operate by day or night, disrupting and wrecking German lines of communication and supply behind the fighting fronts, and destroying any enemy installations or emplacements holding up the Allied armies' advance inland. Once the Allied forces were well established on French soil, the main RAF and USAAF bomber forces returned to their prime task of battering Germany itself; this time with particular concentration upon oil industrial plants and, by night, German cities. Throughout the final year of the war in Europe the bomber offensive increased in sheer weight of bombs released over German targets – and it might be noted that some 75

Left Safely back. Four-man crew of Handley Page Hampden EQ-H, No.408 ('Goose') Sqn, RCAF, on return to Syerston on 30 September 1941, after a sortie. *(Public Archives of Canada)*

Above 'The Beetle wheels his droning flight . . .' – Gray's *Elegy* recalled by a Short Stirling bomber returning from operations at dawn.

per cent of the entire bomb tonnage dropped in the war by the UK-based USAAF was dropped *after* 6 June 1944 – and the bombers continued to support the Allied armies directly by blasting any defences or centres of stiff resistance standing in the armies' path.

By 8 May 1945 – the day declared as VE (Victory in Europe) Day – the RAF had dropped almost one million tons of bombs on German-occupied territories in Europe, while its USAAF partners had contributed another million tons to the awesome weight of destruction. RAF bomber crews throughout the entire war against the Reich had flown a total of almost 390,000 sorties, and lost nearly 8700 aircraft missing on operations.

Going over. Avro Manchester bomber en route to a German target, 1941.

Below 'Time-honour'd Lancaster' – Avro Lancaster NG358 of No.15 Sqn RAF, bearing the yellow fin-markings denoting a *GEE-H* (radar) leader. An example of the best four-engined heavy bomber used by the RAF throughout 1942-5. *(courtesy OC XV Squadron, RAF)*

Right Mother's meeting – Air Vice-Marshal Don Bennett, commander of the RAF's Path Finder Force, 1942-5, chairs the customary morning operations' briefing at PFF Headquarters, Wyton. Behind can be seen that night's projected bomber assault, with routes to and from targets, diversion sorties, *et al* marked with tapes and arrows. *(Sqn Ldr H. Lees)*

Right, below Whatever the weather. Lancasters of No.463 Sqn RAAF at Waddington, near Lincoln, on 1 March 1944.

Left   All aboard for Berlin – Crews of No.77 Sqn RAF (Halifax bombers) about to be transported to their aircraft dispersals prior to another night operation over Germany.

Left, below   Testing their oxygen equipment prior to an operational sortie, a Lancaster crew, skippered by Flight Sergeant R. Martin (left), an Australian from Wards River, New South Wales. *(Pictorial Press)*

Right   S/Sgt Lusic, an aerial gunner of the USAAF's Eighth Air Force. Behind him, 'Meat Hound', a Boeing B-17F of the 423rd Bombing Sqn, 306th Bombardment Group, based at Thurleigh, early 1943. *(USAAF)*

By day . . . Avro Lancaster above a cauldron of smoke and flame during a daylight sortie, 1944.

Below   And by night. Lancasters of No.156 Sqn RAF silhouetted against bundles of dropping target indicator pyrotechnics, over Hanau, on the night of 18/19 March 1945. *(Sqn Ldr H. Lees)*

Below, right   Charlie chased – Lancaster tail gunner ('Arse-end Charlie') about to get grey hairs as a 500lb bomb from a higher aircraft plunges down towards him. In the event, it missed . . . by mere inches. *(Sqn Ldr H. Lees)*

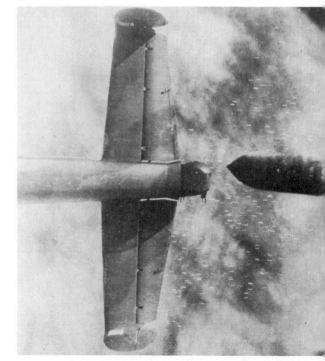

Above Box bombing. Boeing B-17Fs of the 390th BG, 569th B/Sqn, from Framlingham, East Anglia, 'letting go' en salvo over a German target, circa early 1943. *(USAF S. Evans)*

By 1943 all air forces were making increasing use of radar installations, for navigation, bombing and fighter interception. Typical of Luftwaffe radar displays on their defensive fighters was this FuG 202 nose antennae, in a Messerschmitt Bf 110G-4 of NJG/6, which force-landed in neutral Switzerland on 15 March 1944.

Along with the Boeing B-17 'Fortress', the USAAF depended heavily upon the Consolidated B-24 Liberator to maintain the daylight bombing offensive. Here, B-24s from the 467th BG, 8th AF, based at Rackheath, Norfolk, were bombing Landshut on 16 April 1945. *(USAF/M. Bailey)*

Right Precision bombing. A view of Heligoland Bight at 1234 hrs on 18 April 1945, from 19,000 ft altitude, by the crew of Lancaster 'O-Orange' of No.153 Squadron RAF.

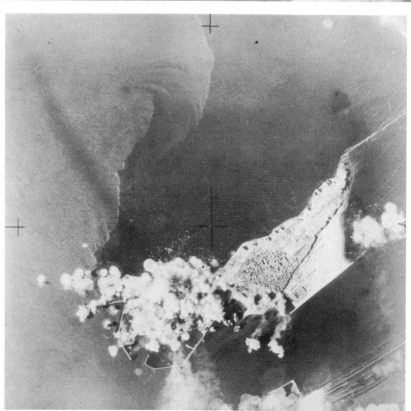

Saturation attack. Aftermath of a bomb raid against the enemy-occupied French airfield of St Cyr.

VIP visit. HM Queen Elizabeth and Princess (now, HM The Queen) Elizabeth visit Lancaster crews of No.15 Sqn RAF at Mildenhall on 5 July 1944.

Below Night scene. Lancaster's view of Hanover on the night of 22 October 1943, with its main Salkstrasse plainly lit up by fires. *(Imperial War Museum, C3898)*

Right Contrails. B-17 Fortresses of the 96th BG, 8th AF, USAAF, based at Snetterton Heath, pound a German objective by day. *(S. Evans)*

Right, below The German Focke Wulf aircraft assembly plant at Marienburg receives 'visiting cards' from B-17 Fortresses of the 390th BG, 8th AF, USAAF, on 9 October 1943. A total of 350 Allied bombers set out for this raid – 28 were lost to enemy defences. *(P. Vance/S. Evans)*

Above The spectacular result of a daylight raid by Halifaxes and Lancasters on an ammunition depot north of Falaise in 1944.

Hero's return. Lt Dalton W. Smith, a B-24 Liberator pilot based in England, jokes with Army Nurse Grace E. Rossiter aboard the hospital ship *Algonquin*, docking at Charleston, USA. Pinned on the wall behind are Smith's gallantry awards of Distinguished Flying Cross, Air Medal, and Purple Heart. Smith's home town was Sacramento, California. *(USA Signal Corps Official)*

Right, above Bomber stream. Part of the force of 359 Lancasters which set out on 25 April 1945 to bomb Adolf Hitler's private chalet, the 'Eagle's Nest', and SS Barracks at Berchtesgaden; seen here among the peaks of the Walchen en route to target. *(Imperial War Museum, CL2673)*

Right, below Reap the whirlwind. A stark view of Essen's bomb damage on 18 May 1945. *(Crown copyright)*

31

Over the Oceans

Right American-built and designed aircraft were supplied in abundance to the RAF throughout 1939-45, including Consolidated Catalina flying boats for ocean patrol and convoy escort operations. Here, Catalina 1b, AX-L, of No.202 Sqn RAF sets out on patrol from Gibraltar, 1941. *(A. Thomas)*

Below Sound & Fury. The sheer bulk of Short Sunderland III, EK591, '2-U', of No.422 Sqn RCAF is gracefully alighted at Castle Archdale base on 15 July 1944. On 10 March of that year, this Sunderland, skippered by Warrant Officer W.F. Morton, had sunk the German submarine U-625. *(Public Archives of Canada)*

The maritime air war of 1939-45 was a vital one for every nation. By that era no country was entirely self-sufficient in the myriad raw materials and other goods necessary to support both domestic usage and industrial production of military items for the war effort. Thus, each nation relied deeply upon imported materials via its own merchant fleet and those of its allies. Equally important was a need to prevent such seaborne sustenance reaching the ports and factories of any opposing nation. Though primarily regarded as a purely naval arena of war, the aircraft of the various nations' maritime forces, originally intended simply for the protection of sovereign coastal waters, were now tasked with operations across the vast oceans of the world; and aerial umbrella, deterrent, and where possible hunter-killers of the lurking wolves of sea warfare – submarines. The RAF's Coastal Command, bolstered by an influx of long-range American-built aircraft, extended its operational range to meet the German U-boat menace in the Atlantic, guarding the helpless merchant ship convoys bringing materials from the USA, and later detached units to cover the South Atlantic, Mediterranean, Red Sea, Persian Gulf and Indian Ocean. Westwards, across the Atlantic, American and Canadian maritime aircraft, home-based, helped to close the gap in aerial cover for the vital convoy routes.

The operational role of maritime crews thus engaged usually entailed hundreds of monotonous flying hours, just 'watching water'; ever-alert for the rare sighting of a U-boat's periscope cutting the oceans surface, or even more rarely, a surfaced submarine. Yet the mere presence of aircraft above or near the convoys was a positive deterrent to many U-boat commanders, these being unwilling to accept the risks inherent with an enemy aircraft nearby, able to deliver instant retribution. The efficacy of maritime aircraft in destroying U-boats may be judged by the following statistics. Of the overall total of 1162 U-boats commissioned in the German Navy, no less than 727 were destroyed by enemy action. Of the latter toll, 288 were sunk by aircraft unaided by

other forces, while a further 47 were sunk at sea in co-operation with Royal Navy ships. It should be added that another 80 were destroyed in base pens by strategic air raids by Allied bombers. The cost of such success for RAF Coastal Command alone amounted to an overall tally of 3500 aircraft lost, and more than 10,000 air crew members killed or injured.

By 1944 coastal aircraft were being reinforced by heavily armed, fast strike aircraft, like the Bristol Beaufighter and all-wood constructed De Havilland Mosquito. Armed with cannons, machine guns, torpedoes, or rockets, these Strike Wings foraged far across the North Sea to Norway and along the European north coastline, seeking out and shattering German merchant convoys, thereby tightening the stranglehold 'blockade' of Hitler's Reich, and denying Germany millions of tons of vital raw materials. This distinctly offensive role was maintained day and night until the final days of the war.

Left Fish porters. The Bristol Beaufighter was not only lethal in designed armament – four 20mm cannons and six machine guns – but highly adaptable, as here, to carry an 18-inch aerial torpedo (known as a 'fish' to its RAF crews) for anti-shipping attacks. *(Bristol Aeroplane Co.)*

Left, below Sea Wolf. The priority enemy hunted was the submarine. Here, the German U-71 is under attack on 5 June 1942 by a Sunderland from No.10 Sqn, RAAF, piloted by Flt Lt S.R.C. Wood. Though claimed as 'destroyed', in fact U-71 managed to limp back to base at La Pallice. *(RAAF Official)*

Below, left Beaufighter EE-C of No.404 Sqn, RCAF, blasts a German *flakschiffe* in the Skagerrack, 15 October 1944. *(Imperial War Museum)*

Below, right Beaufighters of No.143 Sqn, RAF, 'mix it' by cannon and rocket attacks on an enemy merchant convoy, on 22 June 1943 *(Crown copyright)*

Bottom Consolidated B-24 Liberator, KG907, based at Aldergrove, Northern Ireland, on Atlantic patrol, with radome lowered. Of the 350 German U-boats sunk or damaged by RAF maritime aircraft during World War II, Liberators accounted for no less than 100. *(W.V. Cuff)*

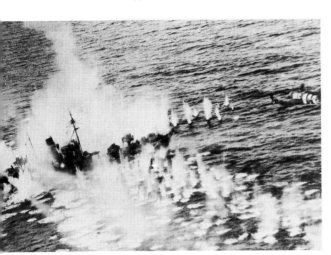

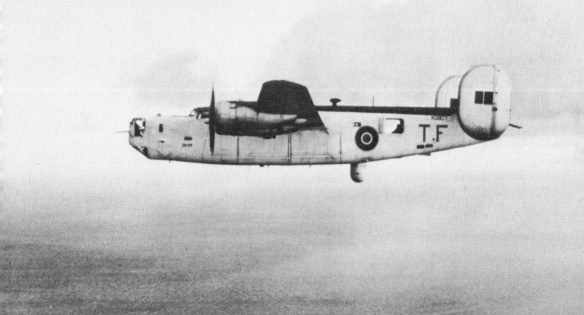

Left Web-foot airmen. Part of the
RAF's coastal forces was the Air Sea
Rescue Service, a mini-navy of sea-
going vessels manned and controlled
by RAF Coastal Command for most of
the war period. No.122 was the first of
the Type 2 Class, known as
'Whalebacks' to their crews, and was
eventually sunk by enemy action
during the Dieppe operation on 19
August 1942. *(Imperial War Museum,
CH2494)*

Left, below Night scene. Anti-
submarine operations were flown
'around the clock' if necessary;
exemplified by this Liberator about to
take off, aided by a ground searchlight
to illuminate the runway. *(Imperial
War Museum, CH14001)*

Right Prize. German U-570 in the
act of surrendering to Lockheed
Hudson, 'S-Sugar' of No.269 Sqn,
RAF, on 27 August 1941. This
submarine was later used by the Royal
Navy, retitled HMS Graph. *(D. Lyall)*

Below Coastal strike. De Havilland
Mosquito 'A', 143 Sqn, RAF, attacking
shipping in Sandefjord, Norway, on
2 April 1945. *(ACM Sir C. Foxley-
Norris)*

Above the Desert

On 10 June 1940 the Italian dictator, Mussolini, declared war on Britain, thereby setting in motion a vast extension of the European conflict; commencing in Africa but eventually embroiling virtually every country bordering on, or in, the Mediterranean zone. At that moment the RAF had just 29 squadrons in RAF Middle East Command. This somewhat misleading title encompassed RAF responsibilities for 'air control' in Egypt, Sudan, Palestine, Trans-Jordan, East Africa, Aden, Somaliland, Iraq, the Balkans, and areas around the Persian Gulf – in geographical terms, a greater area than the United States of America. The meagre RAF force – no more than 300 aircraft – were based mainly in Egypt, but spread thinly around the Command elsewhere. Prime responsibilities were the defence of the Suez Canal, nodal point of access to Britain's far eastern empire; and the island of Malta, strategic key to naval and air power in the Mediterranean.

Though vastly under-strength for such wide responsibilities, and in the main equipped with outdated aircraft, RAF Middle East Command adopted an aggressive attacking role from the outset against the Axis powers in Africa. Though successful initially, the Command was soon weakened by having to detach some squadrons to defend Greece within months of commencing operations, but a successful conclusion to the campaign against Italian forces in Italian East Africa in April 1941 permitted reinforcement units from the latter area to fly north and join the North African war. Strength in aircraft of more modern design in steadily bigger numbers, including many South African and Australian squadrons, enabled the Allied air force to provide effective aerial cover to the hard-pressed infantry of Britain's Eighth Army, which by late 1941 had been pushed eastwards to the border of Egypt by a combined German-Italian land offensive.

For the following year the ground battles along the

North African coastline fluctuated as the opposing armies retreated or advanced, but Allied air strength gradually built up to numerical superiority over the German and Italian opposition, boosted by the receipt of many American-designed fighters and bombers. Liaison between the air and ground forces became highly significant and, by dint of long experience, soon emerged as the key to eventual victory. In October 1942 the battle of Alamein saw the beginning of an Allied advance westwards which eventually routed the Axis forces, and operations in North Africa ceased from May 1943, after the surrender of all remaining enemy troops. Throughout that advance the ubiquity of the desert air forces was evident in the many adaptions of fighter aircraft to become fighter-bombers, tank destroyers, tactical reconnaissance 'eyes', and other diverse roles.

Having defeated the Axis powers in North Africa, the Allied forces, using Malta as a springboard, next invaded Sicily in July 1943, then in early September moved into southern Italy and began advancing northwards. By then enemy air opposition was relatively rare and the Allied air forces, British and American in unison, concentrated on aid to the armies, while USAAF B-24 Liberator bombers based in Italy began raiding southern Germany, thereby dovetailing their raids with those flown from UK bases. The final Allied advance commenced in April 1945, covered by massive (and unopposed) air support, and by 2 May the Italian campaign officially ceased. From the desert air strips of Egypt and Libya, airmen of the desert squadrons had provided unfailing support for the Allied armies through the breadth of North Africa and Tunisia, then Sicily and the entire length of Italy, until victory crowned their prodigious efforts. In doing this they had created a supremely successful fighting partnership of air-ground forces from which matured a fighting combination of arms which proved equally unconquerable in Europe and the jungles of Burma.

Left Early days. A patrol of Gloster Gladiator fighters of No.3 Sqn, RAAF, return to their desert landing ground. *(RAAF Official)*

Above Opposition. Messerschmitt Bf 109E-4/Bs of Jagdgeschwader (JG) 27 over typical North African terrain. *(W.C. Eberhardt)*

Bomber Vic. Trio of Vickers Wellington bombers of No.37 Sqn, RAF, in May 1941; one of the mainstay bombing aircraft of the Allied air forces in the Middle East campaigns.

Right Handley Page Halifaxes of No.462 Sqn RAAF at Messina, August 1943.

Below Sharkmouth. Curtiss P-40 Kittyhawk of No.112 Sqn RAF being guided to take-off point in Libya. The shark's teeth nose marking adapted readily to the engine and propeller boss configuration of this fighter design. *(Imperial War Museum, CM2730)*

Top Briefing. Hurricane pilots of No.6 Sqn RAF being briefed for the day's operations by their commander, Sqn Ldr R. Slade-Betts, DSO, DFC (far left); a daily routine repeated thousands of times on every unit.

Above Maintenance. Curtiss P-40 Kittyhawks of No.450 Sqn RAAF on Malta, mid-1943, being prepared for the imminent Allied invations of Sicily. *(RAAF Official)*

Above Fighter-bomber. Spitfire of No.2 Sqn, SAAF, No.7 SAAF Wing, over the Sangro River, Italy, 1944, fully armed with cannons, machine guns, and a 250lb bomb, for ground attack duties. *(T. Hooton)*

Below 'Save me from my friends.' Liberator B VI, KK320, 'V-Victor' of No.37 Sqn over Montfalcone at 12,500 ft on 16 March 1945. The bombs, from another Liberator 500 ft higher, struck 'Victor' just aft of the cockpit, but – fortunately – did not detonate, and the crippled bomber eventually regained its base safely. *(K. Westrope)*

Left Rocket strike. Beaufighter 'K' of No.16 Sqn, SAAF, of the Balkan Air Force, strafing German barracks at Zuzemberk, Yugoslavia, during the closing months of the war. *(SAAF Official)*

Right B-25 Mitchell bombers of the American 12th Air Force, en route to Cassino, pass Mount Vesuvius in full 'anger'. *(USAF)*

Sheep may safely graze . . . Liberator KG546 of No.70 Sqn RAF at Foggia, Italy, in near-pastoral setting.

Above Mountain men. Spitfire of No.225 Sqn RAF over the Italian Appenines, early 1945.

Right, above Wrecked Heinkel 111 bomber on Catania airfield – symbolic of the Luftwaffe's defeat in the Middle Eastern campaigns.

Right Fallen. An Italian airman's grave, utilising the remains of his Macchi 200 fighter, at El Adem airfield, North Africa.

47

Sea Boots

The 'marriage' of ship and aeroplane can be said to have begun on 18 January 1911 when an American, Eugene Ely, made his first successful landing on the forward deck of the US cruiser *Pennsylvania* in his frail Curtiss biplane; while later generations of aircraft designed to fly from water surfaces owe their origins to a Frenchman, Henri Fabre, who accomplished the world's first aeroplane take-off from water at Martigues, near Marseille, on 28 March 1910. The following three decades saw both facets of maritime aviation progress steadily, albeit slowly, in the major air forces of the world, despite diehard distrust, even opposition among most traditionalist naval hierarchies. By 1939, and the eruption of war in Europe, the flying boat, floatplane, and – most important – aircraft carrier-borne aeroplanes were accepted as an integral part of naval power. If the diehards still reserved judgement upon the worth of such adjuncts to the traditional naval role, such scepticism was quickly to be dispelled within the early war years.

Perhaps the earliest significant feat of arms by naval aircraft to demonstrate conclusively the potential of air power at sea occurred in November 1940, when a handful of obsolete Swordfish biplane torpedo-bombers of the British Fleet Air Arm carrier *Illustrious* crippled the Italian fleet in Taranto harbour, thereby changing the balance of naval supremacy in the Mediterranean. If this bold operation was not sufficient to impress naval authorities, a year later Japanese land-based bombers and carrier-borne aircraft first nullified American naval power in the Pacific by devastating the US fleet vessels in Pearl Harbour; then days later sank the British battleships *Repulse* and *Prince of Wales*. In less than three days, Japanese aircraft had gained undisputed command of Far East waters.

Within the British Fleet Air Arm aircraft specifically designed for naval tasks were overtly outdated at the start of World War II; with the sole exception of the monoplane Skua 'dive-bomber', all contemporary FAA squadrons were flying biplanes of semi-vintage concept. The FAA's total strength in September 1939 was a mere 20 squadrons, comprising some 340 aircraft of all types, though the Royal Navy then owned seven aircraft carriers. Its Allied counterpart, the US Navy, also possessed seven carriers by July 1940, in which month it was authorised to order 11 new aircraft carriers. Germany's navy had only one (of two carriers planned in 1938) the *Graf Zeppelin*, which in the active service; while Japan's relatively modest aircraft carrier strength was never expanded significantly. Britain's lack of home-produced modern maritime aircraft designs was, in the event, to be compensated by a generous flow of American-designed machines for naval use – indeed, until the end of the war the FAA received no British aircraft

Above Stringbag – the universal nickname for the Fairey Swordfish biplane torpedo-bomber used throughout the war by Britain's Fleet Air Arm. This Stringbag is taking off from the carrier *HMS Furious*, loaded (under wings) with depth charges.

Left Cripple. *HMS Ark Royal,* pride of the Royal Navy, attempting to limp to Gibraltar after being torpedoed by the German U-81 on 13 November 1941. She sank under tow the next day. *(Lt-Cdr C.C. Ennever)*

either suitable for carrier work or truly modern in concept; relying primarily on USA Lend-Lease equipment, which by 1945 represented roughly 60-70 per cent of overall FAA strength. By then, May 1945, the Royal Navy had 28 fleet and escort carriers actually at sea, carrying a total of almost 1000 aircraft.

The operational use of naval aircraft borne upon carriers was highly flexible during 1939-45, especially from 1942 onwards in the many Pacific theatre campaigns. Apart from the obvious use of seaborne aircraft to seek out and, possibly, destroy opposing naval forces, the aircraft carrier and its complement came to be employed widely as a floating air base for airborne assaults against enemy land targets – virtually a flying artillery barrage to strike at vital land installations, or to provide a preceding barrage to any attempted seaborne invasion. This latter role continues to the present day as a prime operational *raison d'etre* for the carriers of all navies.

Left, above Escort. Hawker Sea Hurricane being 'recovered' aboard *HMS Victorious*, 1942.

Left Strike force. Fairey Swordfish of *HMS Victorious* waiting to take off for a strike against the German capital ship *Bismarck*, May 1941.
(M. Gidman)

Above Fairey Albacore torpedo-bombers of No.827 Sqn, FAA, from *HMS Indomitable* seeking prey in Far East Waters.

Right Ugly Duckling. The Fairey Barracuda torpedo-bomber – these were from HMS *Indomitable* – supplemented the FAA's Swordfish and Albacore units from early 1943.

Right, below Fairey Fireflies of HMS *Indefatigable* on return from an attack against oil refineries at Pagkalan Brandan, Sumatra, on 4 January 1945.

Yet another American aircraft type used widely by the Fleet Air Arm was the Grumman Martlet (later versions being retitled Wildcat).

Forgotten War

When Japan struck almost simultaneously at the United States of America (Pearl Harbour) and Britain (via Malaya), the focal point of British Far East naval and military forces was Singapore, an island upon which £60 million had been expended in the 1930s to convert it into an 'impregnable fortress'. Yet such lavish finance had not included adequate regard for aerial defences. By December 1941 – when Japan made its moves – the RAF in Malaya comprised a total of 362 aircraft; a motley mixture of obsolete designs, of which no more than two-thirds could even be broadly described as fit for war operations. Airfields were few and lacking reasonable accommodation, maintenance facilities, or defence control systems and radar warning installations. Vastly outnumbered and outclassed by Japanese air opponents, the RAF fought a desperate but losing battle for three months before being forced to abandon Singapore and Sumatra and withdraw to India. Here the survivors faced an advancing Japanese force in Burma intent on conquering India and continued to fight superior odds, including defending Ceylon from a determined Japanese attack in April 1942 which cost the Allies the loss of 15 naval battleships, cruisers and destroyers and the carrier *Hermes*, but failed to capture Ceylon.

The remainder of 1942 for the RAF was a period of recuperation and refurbishment, as sorely needed replacement aircraft were received, albeit mainly second-line types from other equally pressed war theatres. Based mainly around Calcutta, the meagre RAF force was slowly expanded to 26 squadrons by mid-1942, supported by eight squadrons of the Indian Air Force (IAF). By the beginning of 1943 a total of 1443 aircraft were on overall RAF strength, though not all could be considered to be firstline operational types. The same year saw the first expeditions of Orde Wingate's Chindits plunge deep into Japanese-occupied jungle in Burma, supplied and succoured wholly from the air by Dakotas of Nos.31 and 194 Squadrons RAF; a concept of aerial back-up which was to become the key to the eventual Allied triumph in Burma. No longer would the jungle-bound infantry be dependent on land-lines of supply; every item needed would be delivered 'down the chimney' by the indefatigable transport crews in the slow, unarmed aircraft. By the autumn of 1943 the Allied air command in India/Burma could count a total of 48 RAF and 17 USAAF squadrons, figures which would increase to 64 and 28 respectively by May 1944, as the Allies gathered muscle for the ultimate advances through Burma.

If the Allied air crews faced an implacable enemy in the air, they also operated in climatic conditions considered to be the worst in the world. Intensely humid temperatures were relieved (relatively) by seasonal monsoon downpours of rain, while deadly cumulonimbus cloud masses were capable of disintegrating the strongest aircraft, as were the occasional cyclonic winds which could tear a Liberator bomber from its ground-pegging and toss it contemptuously about like a mere toy. The jungle over which the crews flew presented no haven in the event of any forced landing or crash. Within the dark confines of the fetid jungle lurked every known pest and pestilence harmful to human survival apart from a fanatical enemy to whom prisoners of war were merely 'dead men'. Despite all such hazards the RAF and USAAF crews never failed to maintain faith with their comrades below – the so-termed 'Forgotten Army' on the jungle floor.

By June 1944 the Japanese armies had made their last great offensive hoping to gain India, and the Allied forces began to advance through Burma; spearheaded always by RAF and USAAF fighters wreaking havoc with enemy communications and supply lines, while the faithful transport air crews continued their indispensable supply-dropping operations without pause – in February 1945 alone they delivered more than 60,000 tons of food and ammunition to forward elements of the Allied armies. By August 1945 Japanese forces in Burma had been decisively defeated – the 'Forgotten War' (referring to the relative lack of media coverage in Britain for the Burma campaigns) had been won. And the chief ingredient of that victory had been Allied air power. Even at its peak strength the combined British and American air forces in India and Burma had just 48 fighter, 18 bomber, and 24 transport squadrons available; yet a new concept for the use of aerial power had been born and employed in masterly fashion.

Left, above Curtiss Hawk 81A-2 of the famed 'Flying Tigers' group of Americans who flew operations against the Japanese over China, 1940-41.

Left Little Friend. Curtiss Mohawk escort fighter alongside a Douglas Dakota of No.31 Sqn, RAF, over typical Burmese landscape, 1942.

Below The ubiquitous Beaufighter first saw operational use in the India-Burma campaign at Christmas 1942, with No.27 Sqn RAF ('The Flying Elephants'); one of this unit's Beaus seen below in 1945 wearing contemporary South-East Asia Command markings.

Bottom The 'Dak', or Douglas Dakota, was virtually the aerial backbone of the Burma war; providing unfailing and constant supply and transportation support to the 'Forgotten Armies' of the jungle conflict below.

Right Douglas TBD-1 over Wake Island, scene of an heroic stand by the US Marines. At bottom left can be seen Japanese oil stores burning. *(US Navy)*

Right, below Helldriver – the name given to the Curtiss SB2C-4, which was used extensively by US Navy and US Marine Corps units throughout the Pacific operations, 1942-5. *(US Navy)*

Left 'T-Bolt' or 'Jug' were nicknames used for the heavy Republic P-47 Thunderbolt. Though used widely by the USAAF in Europe, the RAF equipped a total of only 16 squadrons with the type, all in the Far East theatre, 1944-6. This example was FL749, 'R' of No.5 Sqn, RAF, in Burma.

Left, below Vought-Sikorsky F4U-1Ds – Corsairs – of a US Marine Corps unit, loaded with 1000lb bomb apiece, head out over the Pacific to a Japanese island target, late 1944. *(US Navy)*

Above Whispering death – the Far East soubriquet for the Beaufighter. This Beau, A8-118, was a Mk XX1 belonging to No.22 Sqn, RAAF. (K.L. Collett)

Left Kamikaze. A Japanese 'suicide' bomber is destroyed before it can achieve its target among an American naval task force. *(US Navy)*

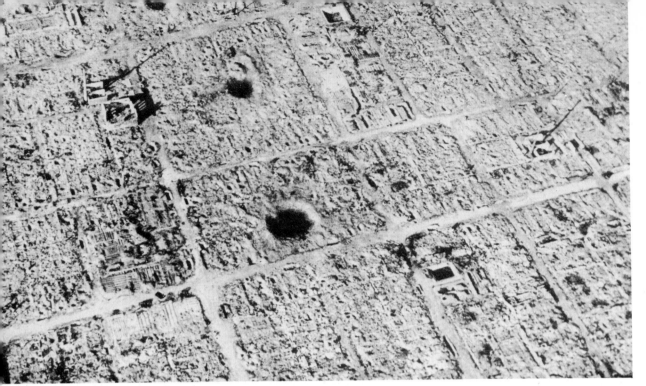

Above Just part of the desolation of Osaka, second city of Japan, after a fire raid (incendiary bombs) by American Boeing B-29 'Superfortresses', 1945. *(USAF)*

Below 'Atomised' Hiroshima – four square miles totally razed by the first atom bomb ever dropped 'in anger', on 6 August 1945. *(USAF)*

Right Deadly mushroom. The second atom bomb to be delivered on Japan by the USAAF fell over Nagasaki on 9 August 1945. This resulting 'mushroom' cloud quickly rose to 45,000 ft. *(USAF)*

Glamour Boys

The fighter pilot – of any air force – has always been regarded, mainly by laymen but even to a degree by fellow air crews – as the glamour boy of military flying. Such an aura originated in the air warfare of 1914-18, when the single-seat scout pilots of Germany, France and the USA were quickly exploited by the popular media as 'aces', i.e. lavish publicity was given to any such pilots claiming five or more combat victories. This 'ace' cult, originated by the French, but soon taken up by German and American journalists and propagandists, was never officially sanctioned within the British air services. Nevertheless, the charisma of the individual knight of the air, engaging in single combat in the skies, flying a gaily coloured fighter aircraft, spread in the layman's imagination to include all such pilots. The years 1918-39 merely increased this legend, when the latest generations of schoolboys and adolescents were inundated with a plethora of magazines and pulp journals, books, films, and model aircraft kits – all laying heavy emphasis on the romantic image of the extrovert, dashing fighter pilot; thereby becoming the ultimate goal of thousands of schoolboys.

The effect of this exploitation was evident in the various air forces of the 1920s and 1930s – indeed, even during the 1939-45 war – when a majority of newly fledged pilots, on graduation from training schools, opted first for postings to fighter units. Once operational, the fighter pilot's image of fulsome glamour continued to be bolstered throughout World War II by the media, and no less by the many extrovert and distinctly individualistic characters whose exploits received lavish coverage. Within the RAF, the outward 'mark' of the fighter pilot was the top tunic button being left unfastened, while many of the more junior pilots often affected distinctly crumpled 'operational' headgear as the badge of their calling. Within the Luftwaffe and USAAF, awards and decorations were liberally showered upon fighter aces, while RAF fighter pilots were (relatively) less generously honoured, and Japanese equivalents received no such 'rewards'. Promotion to senior rank, often at ages unheard of in peacetime, was usually rapid for those fighter pilots who accumulated veteran experience in the early years of the war; 21-year-old Wing Commanders in the RAF were by no means uncommon, while Adolf Galland, the Luftwaffe 'General of Fighters' – an appointment at the age of 30 which had only two superiors, Hitler and Göring – exemplified the combination of youth and experience to be found in most fighter leaders.

The years 1939-45 saw fighter development in most air forces accelerate quickly, starting with biplanes and early monoplane propeller-driven designs and converting to jet-engined or rocket-propelled fighters by 1944. Fighting altitudes rose year by year as bigger and better-powered aircraft were introduced to the combat arena. Combat tactics too altered radically as the war progressed, with increasing emphasis on formation rather than single combat – though once combat was joined, inevitably, most fighter pilots were to a great extent on their own. Attributes vital in any fighter pilot's make-up included keen eyesight, lightning, instinctive reaction to every new situation, self-reliance, and perhaps above all a natural aggressive instinct; that inborn urge to get to grips with an opponent, whatever the circumstances, which was always the hallmark of the 'born' fighter pilot. Fighter combat was always an affair of seconds rather than minutes, a kaleidoscope of physical and mental activities too fast for the human brain to absorb, rationalise, then react at any normal pace. Only the swift survived.

One marked difference between the RAF and USAAF fighter pilots and their German and Japanese opponents lay in the official attitudes of their separate hierarchies to the question of operations. Allied pilots were given specific parameters of sorties or operational flying hours to spells of fighting – 'tours' of operations between which they were 'rested' in non-operational posts; no such relief was available for Luftwaffe or Japanese fighter pilots. Instead they remained on operations until death, injury or promotion removed them from the sharp end of the war; resulting in many German pilots remaining on operations throughout the war and, in many cases, accumulating astonishingly high combat victory scores. Indeed, the highest-scoring fighter ace of all time was a German, Erich Hartmann, with 352 confirmed victories, while no less than 107 Luftwaffe fighter pilots were credited with at least 100 *luftsieg*. In comparison, the highest-scoring RAF ace was a South African, M. St J. Pattle, with at least 41 victories before his death in action; the top USAAF ace was Richard Bong with 40 victories.

Right, above Fighter pilots – and mascot – of No.504 ('County of Nottingham') Squadron, RAF, with one of the unit's Spitfire Vs behind, 1942.

Right Spitfires of No.122 Sqn, RAF, take off from Fairlop airfield (satellite to Hornchurch). (*Imperial War Museum, CH5761*)

Left, above Cheerful pilot and his Messerschmitt Bf 109G-5, employing a 'souvenir' from one of his clashes with USAAF bombers as a back-rest at dispersal.

Left Here they come. Ground crews of No.402 Sqn, RCAF, ready to help their Hurricane pilots at Digby, early 1941. *(Fox Photos)*

Above Hurricane IICs of No.1 Sqn, RAF, diving to attack, circa September 1942.

Left Threading his way through the Russian mud in the winter of 1942-3, a German fighter pilot of JG54 *Grünherz* ('Greenhearts') in a Messerschmitt Bf 109F-2. *(Bundesarchiv)*

Right 'Start!' Focke Wulf Fw 190A-4 of I/JG54 prepares for a sortie on the Russian front, winter 1942-3. *(Bundesarchiv)*

Below Some of the Few. Fighter pilots of No.249 Sqn, RAF, at North Weald, late 1940. From left: P.R.F. Burton, Barton, A.G. Lewis, Crossie, T. Neil, J. Beazley, Sqn Ldr John Grandy (OC Sqn), G. Barclay, K. Lofts.

Above Black beauty. Hurricane IIC, BE500, of No.87 Sqn, RAF, piloted by Sqn Ldr Denis Smallwood, DFC, in nightfighter all-black livery. *(C.E. Brown)*

Naval Captain Dmitriev, decorated with the Order of Lenin, Order of the Red Banner, and a third award for 'Defence of Leningrad'.

Left Night owls. Crew of Mosquito
HR241, 'M', an FBVI version, on
night operations, 3 November 1944.
(Topix)

Left, below Mosquito bite. The
punch of a DH Mosquito's four 20mm
cannons, plus four machine guns
being tested by night on a stop butt.

Right The North American P-51
Mustang, in its later configuration,
was considered by many pilots as the
finest all-round operational Allied
fighter of the war; this example, with
long-range fuel tanks attached, being
from the 357th Fighter Group, 9th Air
Force, USAAF. *(M. Bailey)*

Below Little friend. Republic P-47
Thunderbolt, individually dubbed
'Diablo', with full war-load and
extended-range fuel tank, prepares to
take off for escort duty to its 'Big
Friends' – B-17s and B-24s of the
USAAF bombing Germany. *(Central
Press)*

The Unlucky Ones

the *whole* war period, 1939-45. Comparison with the tolls inflicted upon the Japanese homeland by USAAF B-29 'Superfortresses' during the closing months of the Pacific campaigns bear grim witness to the escalating, awesome destructive power of the aerial weapon. In a *single* raid on Tokyo, on the night of 10

The Service cliché 'War is not a matter of who is right – but who is left', can be applied to every conflict of arms in history. In the context of the air war of 1939-45 it was exemplified tragically. The Royal Air Force, world-wide, suffered totals of 70,253 men and women killed, 13,115 prisoners of war, and a further 22,924 wounded. Of those figures, Bomber Command suffered the highest proportion, with 47,268 air crew members killed in 'non-operational' activities. Fighter Command had 3690 air crew men killed, 1215 others wounded, plus 601 prisoners of war; while Coastal Command operations cost totals of 10,327 air crew men and 1651 ground crew killed, wounded, or injured. The Luftwaffe made equal sacrifices. From 1 September 1939 until 28 February 1945 (the last date for which reliable records are available), a gross total of 44,065 air crew men had been killed or lost on operations, with a further 28,200 sustaining serious, even permanently crippling wounds. 27,610 such air crew men additionally suffered capture as prisoners of war. Although the American forces did not enter the 'lists' until December 1941, the USAAF's losses were grievous. American airmen in the European theatre of operations alone who were killed or died totalled almost 80,000, of which approximately 64,000 were men of the heavy bombers.

The victims of the air war were not confined to those who flew. The bombing operations undertaken by the RAF, USAAF, Luftwaffe *et al* against their opponents' homelands produced horrific tolls of civilians killed or maimed. Although by the nature of such massive destruction, totally accurate figures for overall civilian casualties can even now only be approximations in most cases, the following statistics can be regarded as *minimums*. Allied air raids against territories within the Greater German Reich cost the German civil population a death roll of at least 570,000, apart from 65,000 killed and described officially as 'displaced persons'. Similar statistics for casualties sustained in all forms of aerial assault on the United Kingdom by German forces can be most accurately quoted, amounting to 60,595 killed and 86,182 seriously injured. All such figures applied to

Messerschmitt Bf 109F in the process of destruction by Flight Sergeant Shouldice, an RAF Spitfire pilot. *(Imperial War Museum, C3655A)*

Above   Russian I-153 fighter which crashlanded during the opening phase of Germany's invasion of Russia – 'Operation Barbarossa' – mid-1941.

Top   Heinkel He III victim of Sqn Ldr Adolph Malan, OC 74 Sqn RAF (Spitfires) during the Battle of Britain, 1940. *(Imperial War Museum, C1704)*

Rear turret damage to Short Stirling
'O-Orange' of No.75 (NZ) Sqn RAF
during a raid on Duisburg, 26 April
1943. *(Imperial War Museum, CE58)*

Below Lancaster '*HMT River Spey*'
of No.83 Sqn, RAF, on return from
Germany. *(Wg Cdr R.P. Elliott, DSO,
DFC)*

March 1945, sixteen square miles of the city were gutted by fire – and, by official estimate, more than 130,000 people were killed. The stricken city was to suffer further devastating fire raids within the following weeks. Immediate postwar casualty survey figures issued by officialdom listed totals of over 300,000 killed and a further 350,000 injured as a direct result of aerial bombardment of Japan. Of these, more than one-third died, or were permanently crippled in Hiroshima and Nagasaki – the two cities chosen as the recipients of the first-ever atomic bomb attacks, in August 1945.

Right   An Avro Lancaster suffers a direct hit by flak (anti-aircraft fire) over Germany on 19 February 1945 – seven men have just died. *(Sqn Ldr H. Lees)*

B-24 Liberator victim of Messerschmitt 262 jet fighters on 4 April 1945. It belonged to the 448th BG, 20th Wing, 8th AF, USAAF, based at Seething. *(USAF)*

Kriegie. An RAF air gunner begins
long wearisome years as a
Kriegesgefangener (prisoner of war).
(Imperial War Museum, GER1025)

Below Lancaster of No.115 Sqn RAF
after return to base at Witchford –
minus rear turret and gunner.

Right B-24M Liberator of the 454th BG which had its brakes accidentally applied during take-off run – six men in the nose section were killed instantly. *(USAF)*

B-24 Liberator from the 389th BG, Hethel, the radar leader, goes down in flames during an attack on railway marshalling yards at Munster. *(USAF)*

Halifax B.III, MZ465, MH-Y of No.51 Sqn, RAF, after return from Saarbrucken on 13/14 January 1945 – the result of a mid-air collision. The bomber's navigator and bomb aimer fell out, without parachutes.

Below Boeing B-17 Fortress, *'Hang the Expense'*, on return from Frankfurt on 24 January 1944. The tail gunner, Roy Urich, miraculously escaped by parachute and, though severely wounded, survived as a prisoner of war in Germany. *(USAF)*

Above   A crashed Lancaster, R5845, YW-T, of
No.1660 Heavy Conversion Unit (HCU) being salvaged
for repair. *(Keystone Agency)*

Below   B-24 Liberator of the 460th BG, 15th AF,
USAAF, hit in its fuel tanks by flak over Italy. *(USAF)*

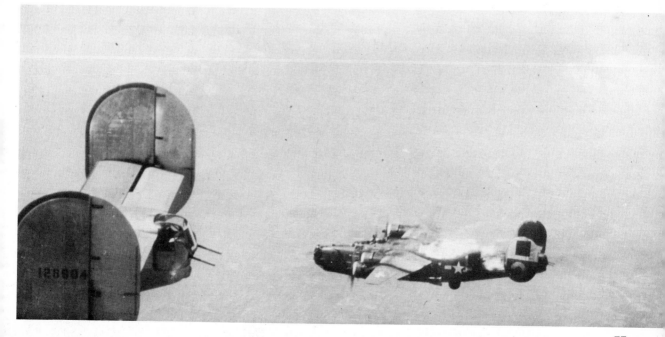

Above B-17 Fortress, 43-38172, of the 398th BG on return to base at Nuthampstead after raiding Cologne on 15 October 1944. A flak shell went through the chin turret, exploded in the bombardier's compartment, killing the bombardier. Note 0.50-inch calibre machine gun still attached to the wreckage. *(USAF)*

Another flak victim – B-24 '*Black Nan*' of 779th BS, 464th BG, 15th AF, USAAF over northern Italy on 9 April 1945. The direct hit threw the bomber over on its back, throwing out Lt E.F. Walsh, the only crew survivor. *(USAF)*

Setting sun. Kawanishi H-97 'Mavis', shot down over the Pacific by a patrolling Liberator.

Douglas A-20 of the 387th Sqn, 312th BG, USAAF, over the Japanese base at Kokas, Bay of Sekar, Netherland New Guinea on 22 July 1944 – seconds before crashing in the sea and killing its crew, Lt J.L. Knarr and S/Sgt C.C. Reichley. (USAF/W.N. Hess)

Douglas A-20J Havoc, 43-10129, of the 416th BG, 9th AF, USAAF, based at Wethersfield, Essex, receives flak in its fuel tanks over France on 12 May 1944. (USAF/W.N. Hess)

The air war of 1939-45 brought together a multi-national host to the ranks of every air force's air crews; a polymorphous blending of races, colours, creeds, and persuasions, having in common only a desire to fly and fight. The Royal Air Force, perhaps, best epitomised most vividly such mixtures of men. To the strictly British national ranks of the RAF after the outbreak of war came a flood of European-born airmen, refugees from Nazi-conquered countries – Polish, Dutch, Belgian, French, Greek – each burning to continue their fighting crusades against Hitler's Germany. They rubbed shoulders daily with men from the British Empire – Australians, New Zealanders, Canadians, and others – and met South Africans, Irish, 'neutral' Americans, Fijians, West Indians, Icelanders – the nationals' roll seemingly endless. Despite such vastly differing backgrounds, cultures, languages, all slotted in to the RAF's routine, especially on the 'sharp end' operational scene.

With rare exception, all such air crews were young – the legal age for majority then was 21 years – but once having been thrown into the crucible of actual operations such youngsters aged rapidly in the mental context. A few months, weeks, even days of life-and-death aerial conflict swiftly ripped away the pseudo-glamorous mask of 'air combat' perpetuated in pulp

Above Lieutenant Edward Henry O'Hare, USN, who shot down five Japanese aircraft in a single combat on 20 February 1942, and was awarded a Congressional Medal of Honor for this feat. His subsequent tally of victories totalled twelve. *(US Navy)*

Right Flying Officer Edgar James – 'Cobber' – Kain, DFC, who served with No.73 Sqn RAF in France, 1939-40, claimed 17 victories – the RAF's first fighter ace of the war – but was killed in a flying accident on 7 June 1940 in France. A New Zealander, he joined the RAF in 1936.

Pilot Officer Stanley Michel Kolendorski, an American of Polish extraction from Bell, California, who joined No.71 Sqn, RAF – the first American 'Eagle Squadron' – in November 1940, but was killed in action on 17 May 1941; the first 'Eagle' to die by enemy action.

Flying Officer (later, Sqn Ldr) T.N. Scholefield, RAAF, of No.467 Squadron RAAF, 1944, who hailed from Cryon, New South Wales, Australia.

magazine and Hollywood epic, revealing the ugly face of death or mutilation. From that moment of realisation most air crews had one prime goal – kill or be killed, the primitive truism of survival. Off-duty, many young air crews lived at a high pitch of hedonistic activities – 'Live for today, tomorrow may never come' was an all-too accurate motto for many men. Other crews, often slightly older, men with wives and children, preferred to concentrate their energies into 'the job' – and to survival.

If the 'Grim Reaper' – an RAF euphemism for death – was a constant companion on operations, there was humour too, and the tight-knit bond of comradeship inherent in any community sharing a common peril. Total strangers, from all levels of social standing, were brought together within a squadron, then quickly, necessarily, welded themselves into a cohesive fighting whole – exemplified particularly among the bomber crews, whose inter-dependency was the only real hedge against the 'chop'. For many thousands of those youngsters their aircraft eventually became their last tangible link with life. Like the epitaph to the dead of Kohima, they 'gave [their] tomorrow for [our] today' . . .

Above Wing Commander (later, Air Commodore, Sir) Hughie Idwal Edwards, VC,DSO,DFC, born in Australia of Welsh immigrant parents, who joined the RAF in 1936.

Above, right Polish fighter aces of the Battle of Britain. L-R: Sqn Ldr Witold Urbanowicz, Fg Offs Jan Zumbach and Miroslaw Feric, Flt Lt Zdzislaw Henneberg. Pictured on 15 December 1940 when all received a British Distinguished Flying Cross (DFC) award for their prowess.

Flight Lieutenant 'Tiny' Hunter, DFC (left), an ex-Metropolitan Police heavyweight boxing champion who stood 6ft 5in tall, was a Catalina skipper with No.240 Sqn, RAF. *(British Official)*

Left Squadron Leader Jean E.F. Demozay, DSO,DFC, a Frenchman who claimed a total of 21 combat victories before being killed in a flying accident on 19 December 1945.

Wing Commander Blair Dalzel Russel, DSO,DFC, from Montreal, Canada, who fought in the Battle of Britain, and remained on fighter operations throughout the war. *(British Official)*

Far left Wing Commander Richard Maxwell Milne, DFC, a Scot who claimed 15 combat victories before being shot down on 20 January 1943, and becoming a prisoner of the Germans. The strain of operations is evident on his young face.

Left Air Vice-Marshal Donald C.T. Bennett, CB,CBE,DSO,AFRAeS, the Australian-born commander of the RAF's Path Finder Force from its inception in August 1942 to 1945.

Left Polina Ossipenko, a Russian female air ace who, with Valentina Grizodubova in 1937, had established a long-distance record flight from Moscow to California.

Right Lt-Colonel B.F. Safanov, one of the first Russian aces to fly Hawker Hurricanes. He was killed in action in May 1942.

Lt-Commander Eugene Esmonde, VC,DSO,RN who died leading six Fairey Swordfish torpedo-bombers attempting to attack the German battleships *Scharnhorst, Gneisenau* and *Prinz Eugen* in the English Channel on 12 February 1942. *(Lt-Cdr C.C. Ennever)*

Below Luftwaffe *Experten* ('aces'), including, in white jacket, Adolf Galland, who was later promoted to General of Fighters.

Left Group Captain Adolph Gysbert Malan, DSO,DFC – 'Sailor' – a South African, who claimed at least 35 combat victories, and was acknowledged as probably the RAF's finest fighter leader of 1939-45. He survived the war but died of Parkinson's disease on 17 September 1963. *(Imperial War Museum, CH12859)*

Above Colonel Charles Lindbergh, of solo-trans-Atlantic flight fame (left) with Major T.B. McGuire, Jr, the USA's No.2 fighter ace (38 victories) at Hollandia air strip, Dutch New Guinea, June 1944. *(D. Glenn Cooper)*

Left Flight Lieutenant George Beurling, DSO,DFC,DFM – 'Buzz' or 'Screwball' to his friends – achieved fame as a Spitfire pilot on Malta in mid-1942, claiming 27 victories in just two weeks' desperate fighting. A Canadian from Verdun, Quebec, he was killed in an aircraft crash at Urbe airport, Rome, on 20 May 1948 while engaged in ferrying aeroplanes to Israel.

Lt-Colonel Leon Vance, USAAF, whose courage on only his second operational mission with the 489th BG, Eighth AF, in a B-24H, on 5 June 1944, led to the award of a Congressional Medal of Honor. The award was, however, made posthumously, after Vance and the aircraft in which he was being flown back to the United States disappeared without trace on 26 July 1944. *(USAF)*

Right Group Captain Frank – 'Chota' – Carey, DFC,AFC,DFM, whose ultimate officially credited victory score of 28 is considered by most contemporaries to be a gross underestimation of his true tally. *(Imperial War Museum, CI171)*

Right, below Hurricane pilots of No.28 Sqn, RAF, in Burma, circa 1943-4. *(Imperial War Museum, CF368)*

Below Ace meets king. HM King George VI talking informally with a Spitfire pilot immediately after his return from a sortie over France on 29 April 1942. On the pilot's cheeks can be seen the facial creasing caused by his rubber oxygen/microphone nose-piece. *(Associated Press)*

Heraldry of Combat

The marking of all military aircraft with insignia indicating nationality was first agreed by the ordinances (as later amended) of the 1907 Hague Convention; a 'legal' authority and responsibility which passed to the International Court of Justice, an integral facet of the newly created United Nations Organisation (UNO), in 1945. Each nation's officialdom next decreed the 'proper' methods and means of depicting national origin, and extended such markings by issuing, from time to time, the latest official unit or squadron identification systems. After the 1914-18 war most military aircraft units were eventually awarded official, heraldic unit badges or crests, often bearing motifs and mottos of peculiar significance to individual units, e.g. certain RAF squadrons' badges bore motifs depicting particular animals – an elephant or a camel, perhaps – which recalled the actual names of aircraft equipping the squadron when it was originally formed. Thus, such items could provide a continuing link in the chain of any unit's traditions from one generation of crews to all others who served with that specific squadron, thereby providing and fostering an esoteric pride in membership.

However, with the natural perverseness of man, from almost the very beginning of military aviation history, individual pilots and crews have sought to single out their squadron and personal aircraft from all others by embellishing the latter – usually without official approval – with distinctive insignia additional to the mundane official markings. This desire to be identified as an individual, rather than just another number, is part of the human character, and

represented a modern equivalent of the medieval practice of barons and other knightly nobles displaying private shields and banners or insignia in battle. The aerial war of 1939-45 saw this practice of personal aircraft identification spread widely among almost every facet of every air force involved. Fighter pilots in particular, in keeping with their highly individualistic role, often emblazoned their personal 'steeds' with private 'victory logs' of enemy aircraft claimed as destroyed; while bomber crews occasionally painted up similar 'logs' of successfully completed bombing sorties or missions.

Of the three major air forces engaged in the air war – the RAF, USAAF, and Luftwaffe – the RAF was

perhaps the most modest in applying such displays, but the USAAF was certainly the most extrovert. By 1943 most American operational aircraft, particularly fighters and bombers, carried virtual minor works or art alongside cockpits and engine cowlings. The more military-minded, discipline-conscious Luftwaffe hierarchy, while permitting certain high-scoring *experten* ('aces') to record *luftsieg* (victory) tallys, usually on the tail or rudder, also ordered the painting of large areas of some fighters, e.g. nose sections in bright, easily seen colour schemes to aid rapid identification by fellow pilots during the turmoil of combat, an inherited tradition from the more gaudy aircraft markings borne by their forebears' aircraft in the German Imperial Air Services of 1914-18.

If more sedate officials frowned upon such glamourising, they usually remained silent, recognising the psychological advantages in the context of morale among such crews; while those media outlets concerned with boosting the morale of a nation's civilian population seized gladly on such overt light-hearted markings as 'good copy'.

Left Fighting cocks. Sqn Ldr D.L. du Vivier, the Belgian commander of No.43 Sqn RAF (3rd from right) watching his pilots affixing a large adaption of the squadron's official badge to his Hurricane.

Above RAF airmen removing the 'Hades Cupid' insigne from a Messerschmitt Bf 109E of 2/JG52 which was shot down near Berwick, Sussex, on 12 August 1940.

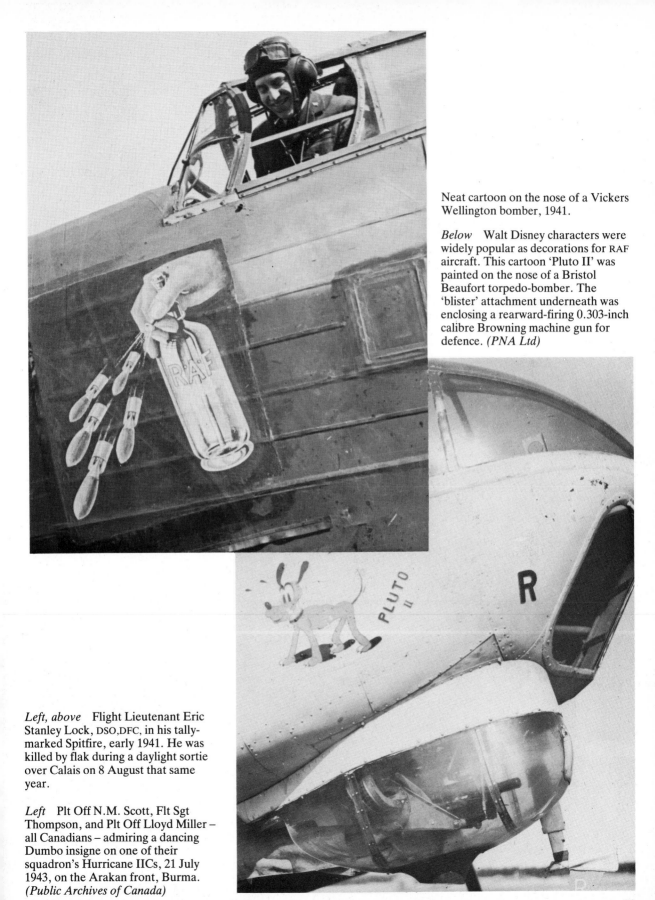

Neat cartoon on the nose of a Vickers Wellington bomber, 1941.

Below Walt Disney characters were widely popular as decorations for RAF aircraft. This cartoon 'Pluto II' was painted on the nose of a Bristol Beaufort torpedo-bomber. The 'blister' attachment underneath was enclosing a rearward-firing 0.303-inch calibre Browning machine gun for defence. *(PNA Ltd)*

Left, above Flight Lieutenant Eric Stanley Lock, DSO,DFC, in his tally-marked Spitfire, early 1941. He was killed by flak during a daylight sortie over Calais on 8 August that same year.

Left Plt Off N.M. Scott, Flt Sgt Thompson, and Plt Off Lloyd Miller – all Canadians – admiring a dancing Dumbo insigne on one of their squadron's Hurricane IICs, 21 July 1943, on the Arakan front, Burma. *(Public Archives of Canada)*

Far left Vought-Sikorsky F4U-I Corsair from the US Navy unit VF-17, known irreverently as 'Blackburn's Irregulars' after a unit commander, Captain John T. Blackburn, displaying the unit's black/white skull and crossbones insigne. This particular Corsair 'belonged' to Ensign Ira Kepford, whose eventual 'score' of 17 officially confirmed victories made him the fifth highest ranking US Navy fighter ace of World War II. Photo taken on 15 April 1944. *(Imperial War Museum/*US *Navy)*

Left Sqn Ldr I. Kilmartin, DFC, an ex-veteran of the 1939-40 French campaign, in his tally-inscribed Hurricane fighter in West Africa, early 1942.

Left The 203rd 'sortie completed' bomb is painted on the log of De Havilland Mosquito LR503, GB-F, 105 Sqn, RAF, while Flt Lt T.P. Lawrenson (pilot) and Flt Lt D.W. Allen, DFC (navigator), look on. The Mosquito ultimately recorded 213 sorties, but crashed into Calgary Airport on 10 May 1945 during a flying display tour of Canada. *(Sqn Ldr H. Lees)*

Above Grim reaper – the grisly 'badge' of DH Mosquito IV, DK333 of No.109 Sqn RAF, with its contemporary bomb 'log' showing 29 sorties completed. *(Wg Cdr F. Ruskell, DFC)*

Left   Personal markings on most Allied aircraft were relatively modest, exemplified here by the Spitfire flown by Wg Cdr J.J. Le Roux, DFC, a 24-victory ace from South Africa, who died in a flying accident on 19 September 1944.

Left, below   Wing Commander Brendan Finucane, DSO,DFC, seated in his No.452 Sqn RAF Spitfire. The monogrammed shamrock betrays Finucane's land of birth, Ireland.

Above   Group Captain F.D.S. Scott-Malden, DFC, in a 'presentation' Spitfire.

Below   Joker. Squadron Leader John W.C. Simpson, DFC, commander of No.245 (Hurricanes) Sqn, RAF, late 1940. *(British Official)*

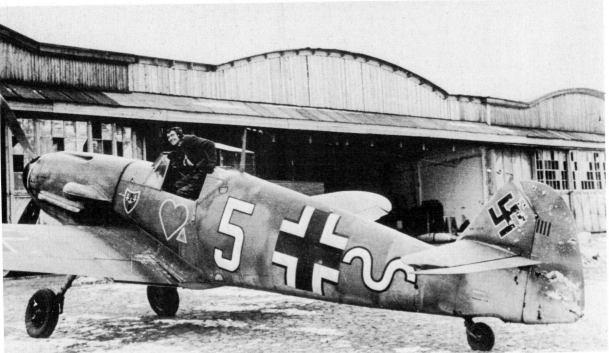

Top Luftwaffe fighter pilots customarily displayed *Luftsieg* ('victories') on the tails of their aircraft, as here on the Focke Wulf Fw 190 of Leutnant Joseph 'Sepp' Wurmheller, *Staffelkapitan* of 9/JG2.

Above Messerschmitt Bf 109F-2 of JG54 *Grünherz* ('Greenhearts') on the Russian front, displaying combat damage to its tail.

Right Insigne inspired by an internationally known Scotch whisky advertisement on the nose of Lancaster W4964, 'J' of No.9 Sqn, RAF. The bomb log shows 104 operations completed to date. Other markings include eight medal ribbons, an enemy aircraft and searchlight destroyed, war service chevrons; while the small kangaroo further aft indicated an Australian navigator's compartment. *(Sqn Ldr T. Mason)*

Above Hoist by his own petard. A quote from a boastful speech by the Luftwaffe supremo, Hermann Göring, was proudly painted below the impressive sorties' bomb log of Lancaster B.1, R5868, PO-S, 'Sugar', of No.467 Sqn, RAAF. Note 'awards' of one DSO and two DFC ribbons at foot of log. Pilot here is Pilot Officer J.W. McManus from Nedlands, Perth, Australia. This actual aircraft is now (1983) permanently preserved in the Royal Air Force Museum, Hendon, near London.

Left A Mosquito's markings combined Donald Duck with playing cards, with the 'motto', *'Knave of Diamonds'*; the 'personal' aircraft of Wing Commander John de L. Wooldridge, DSO,DFC,DFM, commander of No.105 Sqn RAF, June 1943. *(Hawker-Siddeley Aviation)*

Above *Le Grand Charles* – 'personal' Hawker Tempest fighter of the French ace, Sqn Ldr Pierre Clostermann, DFC, of No.3 Sqn RAF, 1945.

Below Even when the war was over, the habit persisted for a period, as on this Vickers Warwick V, LM837, 'Y', viewed at Fayid, Egypt, circa 1946.

They also Served-the Erks

Perhaps more than 90 per cent of all published literature on the air wars of this century has featured the men who actually flew: pilots, navigators, bombardiers, gunners, *et al.* As the sharp end of every air force, this emphasis is not only logical but, in the main, justified. Nevertheless, it should be recognised that actual air crews represent a relatively small proportion of every aerial service. For every flying Serviceman, there existed 40 or 50 non-flying men and women, each providing a vital link in the massive 'support' services necessary to maintain aircraft and air crews for their primary role. Of the major air services involved in the 1939-45 war, the Royal Air Force offers, probably, the most significant view of such ground crews. This was because, unlike

most of the other air forces, ground personnel in the RAF had always been comprised in the main of men on long-term, 'regular' engagements – 'career' men who had joined the RAF at ages from 15 to 19 years and 'signed on' to complete long, even pensionable terms of service. When war erupted in 1939, and the necessary, rapid expansion of numbers of personnel became vital, their ranks were swelled enormously by men and women who volunteered (or, later, were conscripted) for 'duration of hostilities' only. By early 1943, their number exceeded one million men and women in non-flying capacities; some 80-odd per cent of whom were on non-regular service engagements.

They came from the furthest corners of the globe, particularly those countries and colonies which – then – comprised the massive British Empire; each eager to 'do their bit' for the Mother Country, Britain. The RAF, in its mysterious wisdom, placed a majority of such men and women in ground trades totally divorced from any previous experience or expertise, yet all coped and persevered with their allotted niche in the overall scheme of things. Such men and women also derived from all classes and strata of civilian society, 'rubbing shoulders' and merging into a cohesive whole in the common cause of winning the war.

Their conditions of service were seldom sinecures. Pay and allowances for 'Erks' – the universal soubriquet for all non-commissioned personnel within the RAF – were minimal. Living conditions could vary from the relative luxury of a peacetime-

built barrack block on a permanent station, to a rusting, roughly sited Nissen hut or even tent, devoid of proper heating, drainage, or toilet facilities, situated miles from 'civilisation'. Working hours' parameters were – at least, on operational flying units – non-existent; 'the job' took priority over all matters and often meant working throughout a full seven-days' week, for weeks, even months at a time. A posting abroad to any overseas theatre of war usually meant a total absence from kith and kin for several years. And once overseas the Erk was – too often – a victim of the lingering prewar class-snobbery by resident populations; a 'second-class citizen' whose entry to the more fashionable places of accommodation, refreshment or entertainment was forbidden by higher authorities – such places were for 'Officers Only' . . . .

Left Armourers of No.38 Sqn, RAF, in Libya, 1942, in typical desert campaign variety of 'uniform'. *(L. Jordan)*

Above Leading Aircraftmen (LACs) J. Holland and P. Laroche, Corporal L. Lott, and LAC H. McGuiniss, apply muscle-power to lifting a 250lb high explosive bomb onto its wing-carrier, on a Hurricane IIB fighter-bomber of No.402 Sqn, RCAF, at Warmwell, 9 February 1942. *(Public Archives of Canada)*

In the main, however, such snobbery of 'class distinction' was not to be found at the sharp end – the first-line squadrons. There, air crews and ground crews were united by a common respect for each other's role. Most air crews recognised that the aircraft in which they flew to war depended entirely upon the Erks' skills, efficiency, and unbidden devotion; thus the air crews' lives were, to a great extent, in the hands of their faithful ground crews. For their part, the Erks reciprocated this trust by sparing no effort in ensuring that 'their' aircraft was always 100 per cent fit for operations if humanly possible. All successes and other achievements of the air crews were celebrated in equal measure by their own Erks – a commonality of pride in which each indicated their full appreciation of the other's part.

It might be thought that, being on the ground, the Erks had, at least, a safe occupation in the context of war operations. Such was not the case. Taking the RAF alone, by the cessation of hostilities in August 1945, no less than 9700 Erks had been killed on active service, a further 6561 wounded or severely injured, while 4500 had suffered as prisoners of war; a total amounting to almost one-fifth of *all* RAF casualties throughout the war. Perhaps their most apt epitaph are John Milton's words, 'They also serve who only stand and wait' . . . .

Above Corporal 'Fergie' Ferguson (right) supervises a bowser refuelling for a Lancaster of No.57 Sqn RAF at East Kirkby. *(Sqn Ldr H.B. Mackinnon, DFC)*

Right Rearming the wing-guns of a Hurricane, and replenishing its fuel tanks between sorties. *(Imperial War Museum, CH3782)*

Right With its pilot in the cockpit, this Hawker Typhoon of No.247 (*'China-British'*) Sqn, RAF, is loaded with its battery of eight 3-inch rocket projectiles in France, shortly after the initial Allied invasion of France in June 1944. *(Imperial War Museum, CL160)*

Tall tale. A Fabric Worker repairs damage to the tail of a Short Sunderland flying boat; a job obviously needing a head for heights. The Sunderland, DA-J, belonged to No.210 Squadron, RAF. *(Imperial War Museum, CH858)*

Right Tropical troubles. Scene at Koggala, Indian Ocean, which became a flying boat maintenance base for Far East Theatre maritime operations; in this case Short Sunderland undergoing engine changes. *(British Official)*

Right, below Groundcrew maintenance was inevitably similar in all air forces. In this view, Luftwaffe mechanics are rearming the wing guns of a JG54 Messerschmitt Bf 109F.

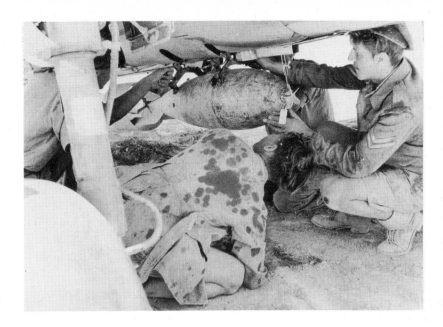

Right Oil-stained and sand-encrusted, three armourers lock a 250lb HE bomb to a Curtiss P-40 Kittyhawk of No.112 ('*Sharkmouth*') Sqn of the Desert Air Force, North Africa, 1942. *(Imperial War Museum, CM2898)*

Left Whatever the weather. A Messerschmitt Bf 109E gets an overhaul in North Africa, under a baking, daily sun.

Below Beaufighter of No.252 Sqn, RAF, receiving a major inspection against a background of palms and sand, Libya.

Left Lapping in the machine gun ammunition belts to the nose guns of a 613 Sqn, RAF, DH Mosquito FB VI. *(Flight photo)*

Right Refuelling a Focke Wulf Fw 190A-4 of the 7 Staffel, III/JG2, 'Richthofen'. *(Bundesarchiv)*

Below Sqn Ldr R.E. Morrow, DFC, a Canadian who commanded No.402 Sqn, RCAF, watches his Hurricane IIB, BE417, AE-K, being bombed up at Warmwell, early 1942. Note doped fabric patches over the wing guns' ports to keep out dust until the moment of first firing.

Left, above Food of war. An armament mechanic of the Women's Auxiliary Air Force (WAAF) running belts of 0.303-inch calibre ammunition through a positioning machine, prior to issue to Lancasters of No.619 Sqn, RAF, on 14 February 1944. *(Imperial War Museum, CH12285)*

Above Bombing-up, particularly 'heavy' bombers, meant hours of sheer muscle-straining labour; exemplified here by 'Erks' of No.405 Sqn RCAF positioning a trolley-load of 1000lb He bombs under Handley Page Halifax 'Q-Queenie'. *(Imperial War Museum, CH6609)*

Left Wheeling in a 4000lb high capacity (HC) bomb – a 'Cookie' – under the bomb bay of DH Mosquito PF432, 'W' of No.128 Sqn, RAF, at Wyton on 21 March 1945, prior to a raid on Berlin.

caption overleaf

Previous page Servicing commandos – the official title for 'selected' technical tradesmen who accompanied squadrons to France with the initial Allied invasion of Normandy from 6 June 1944. Spitfires of Nos. 332 (AH), 411 (DB), and 56 (US) Squadrons of the 2nd Tactical Air Force (TAF) provide a backcloth to armourers belting boxes of 20mm cannon shells. *(PNA Ltd)*

Right Critical ears as two engine fitters listen to the engines of Halifax LL126, 'W', during a ground-run after servicing. *(Imperial War Museum; CH12526)*

Far right Needs must. Improvised 'working platform' for engine mechanics working on a Hurricane fighter in Egypt, 1941. *(PNA Ltd)*

Below 'Come ahead both' – an airframe mechanic marshalling a 613 Squadron DH Mosquito at Lasham, 1944. *(Flight photo)*

Right, below Without self-power, any aircraft is simply a heavy object. Luftwaffe mechanics use 'natural' means of repositioning a Messerschmitt Bf 109 into its servicing 'bay'.

Above Cannon-fodder. Lapping in the belts of 20mm cannon shells for a Hurricane IIC. Note each cannon's spring-loaded Belt Feed Mechanisms (BFMs) ready for connection to each belt.

Medals – or 'Gongs' in RAF parlance – were rarely awarded to non-flying crewmen. One of the exceptions was this award by HM King George VI of a British Empire Medal (Military Division) to Flight Sergeant B.H. Hornden on 16 January 1941.
(PNA Ltd)

Above Night-shift. There were no normal working hours for the Erks, or 'unsociable hours'; every day meant work at any time necessary. The job came first in all things.

Typical dispersal scene while DH Mosquito of No.464 Sqn undergoes maintenance at Hunsdon, 1944. *(Hawker-Siddeley Aviation)*

The Forces' sweetheart – Vera Lynn
in an informal moment with the crews
of No.31 Squadron RAF (Dakotas),
Agartala, Burma, in May 1944.
(31 Squadron Association)

BIBLIOGRAPHY

Any attempt to catalogue the plethora of books and other literature pertaining to the aerial war of 1939-45 would, necessarily, require many weighty volumes. The following selected titles are simply this author's subjective choice of some of the better basic reference works and occasional specifically detailed accounts of the more significant facets of that conflict.

Royal Air Force, 1939-45, 3 vols, Richards/Saunders, HMSO, 1952
Strategic Air Offensive against Germany, 4 vols, Webster/Frankland, HMSO, 1961
Defence of the United Kingdom, B. Collier, HMSO, 1957
Bomber Offensive, A.T. Harris, Collins, 1947
History of the RAF, 1912-78, C. Bowyer, Hamlyn, 1977
Fighter Command, 1936-68, C. Bowyer, Dent, 1980
Air War over Europe, 1939-45, C. Bowyer, Kimber, 1981
For Valour – The Air VCs, C. Bowyer, Kimber, 1978
Guns in the Sky – Air Gunners, C. Bowyer, Dent/Corgi, 1979/81
The Narrow Margin, Wood/Dempster, Arrow, 1969
The Desert Air Force, R. Owen, Hutchinson, 1948
The Central Blue, J. Slessor, Cassell, 1956
Briefed to Attack, H.P. Lloyd, Hodder & Stoughton, 1949
2nd Tactical Air Force, C.F. Shores, Osprey, 1970
Wings of the Phoenix, HMSO, 1949
Photo-Reconnaissance, A.J. Brookes, Ian Allan, 1975
Instruments of Darkness, A.W. Price, Kimber, 1967

Wings of the Morning, I. Cameron, Hodder & Stoughton, 1962
Fiasco, J.D. Potter, Heinemann, 1970
Destiny can wait, PAF Association, Heinemann, 1949
Destruction of Dresden, D. Irving, Kimber, 1963
The night Hamburg died, M. Caidin, Ballantine, 1960
Carrier Operations, 2 vols, D. Brown, Ian Allan, 1968/74
The Greatest Air Battle – Dieppe, N. Franks, Kimber, 1979
The Guinea Pig Club, E. Bishop, Macmillan, 1963
Eagle Day, R. Collier, Dent, 1980
RCAF Overseas, 3 vols, OUP, Toronto, 1944-9
RAAF Official History, 4 vols, AWM, 1954-63
SAAF History, 3 vols, Brown/Martin/Orpen, Purnell, 1970-7
History of Indian Air Force, Official, 1961
New Zealanders with the RAF, 3 vols, WHB, NZ, 1953-9
The Mighty Eighth, R. Freeman, Macdonald & Jane's, 1970
Mighty Eighth War Diary, R. Freeman, Jane's, 1981
The US Strategic Bomber, R. Freeman, Macdonald & Jane's, 1975
Black Thursday, M. Caidin, Ballantine, 1966
Big Week, G. Infield, Pinnacle, USA, 1974
Pacific Sweep, W. Hess, Doubleday, 1974
A Torch to the Enemy, M. Caidin, Ballantine, 1960
Rise & Fall of the German Air Force, Air Ministry, 1948
Birth of the Luftwaffe, H. Schliephake, Ian Allan, 1971
Luftwaffe – An Analysis, Ed. H. Faber, Sidgwick & Jackson, 1979
The Luftwaffe War Diaries, G. Bekker, Macdonald, 1966
The First & the Last, A. Galland, Methuen, 1955
V2, W. Dornberger, Hurst & Blackett, 1954
The Mare's Nest, D. Irving, Kimber, 1964
History of the German Nightfighter Force, G. Aders, Jane's, 1979
The Soviet Air Force, A. Boyd, Macdonald & Jane's, 1977
Zero, Okumiya/Horikoshi/Caidin, Cassell, 1957